The Lord will send His faithful love by day;
His song will be with me in the night—
a prayer to the God of my life.
—Psalm 42:8

To

From

On this date

Dedication

This book is dedicated to our parents, Larry and Rhonwyn Kendrick,
who modeled the power of prayer for us growing up.
We would stumble upon our dad on his knees in his closet
or by the bed praying for our family.
Our mother still gets up early every morning
and prays for her children and grandchildren by name.
Words cannot express how much you mean to us, Mom and Dad.
We love you and thank God for you!
May your legacy of faith live on for many generations.

Peter's Perfect Prayer Place

Stephen Kendrick and Alex Kendrick

illustrated by Daniel Fernández

B&H KIDS

Nashville, Tennessee

My mommy's in her prayer room
Where she loves to talk with God.
She likes to pray for everything—
For me and dad and Todd.

She thanks God for the good things
That I am doing right,
Like how I'm learning to obey
And ate all my beans last night.

I wish I had a special place
Where I could go pray too.
The perfect place ... Where should I go?
I just don't know. Do you?

Maybe in the kitchen
Where my mommy goes to cook.
I need somewhere to talk with God.
Will you come help me look?

Take a peek at what I see.
I think I might have found it!
Beneath the stove there is a space
With lots of pots around it.

I'll sneak right in the middle
With a snack and drink each day
And talk to God while I'm inside.
Can this be where I pray?

Oh, no! These pans are clanging
And way too loud already.
And what if Mommy needs these pots
To make soup or pasketty?

How will I pray when Mommy cooks?
It's not where I should be. . . .
And what if the kitchen starts to smell
Like fish or broccoli?

Yippee! In here is better,
And this tent is just my size.
When I pray, I'll wear my helmet
To protect me from bad guys.

But I can't find the light switch,
And Todd looks dark and gray.
Does God still hear me in the dark?
Whose bright idea was this anyway?

My backyard is much better!
I can see and breathe fresh air.
God can watch me while I swing
And hear my every prayer.

But it's really busy out here,
Lots of noises in this world.
I might not pray much in this swing—
Hey, look! There goes a squirrel!

Or maybe that's my special place—
To pray there on that limb.
I'll climb up higher, close to God,
And sing a song to Him.

But I don't want to slip up there.
I'll stay on the ground instead.
I'm really not afraid of heights. . . .
Just of falling on my head!

Back in my bed's the place to pray!
It's safe and not too high.
And I can talk to God while
Undercover like a spy.

My pillow's soft. It's not too loud.
And—*yawn*—my sheets are warm.
This is where I'll talk to God
About my . . . um . . . um . . . ZZZZZZZZZZZZZZZZ

One hour later . . .

Hey, what happened? Where am I?
I think I fell asleep!
I wanted to be praying,
But instead I counted sheep.

Inside, outside, underneath—
Just where will God be near me?
How do I find the perfect place
Where He will really hear me?

Then Daddy says, "It's great to pray
And have a favorite place,
Like kneeling by your bed
Or another quiet space.

    "But God can see and hear you, son,
    No matter where you pray!
    You can talk to Him from anywhere,
    At any time of day."

Wow, God! I didn't know that
You hear me all the time!
With such a perfect God like You,
Each place I pray is fine.

I think I'll pray here in my room
Though you're with me when I leave.
'Cause where I am is where You are,
And that's the perfect place for me!

You are aware of all my ways.
Before a word is on my tongue,
You know all about it, LORD.
—Psalm 139:3–4

"Let the little children come to Me.
Don't stop them, for the kingdom of God
belongs to such as these."
—Mark 10:14

Remember:

"But when you pray, go into your private room, shut your door, and pray to your Father who is in secret. And your Father who sees in secret will reward you."—Matthew 6:6

Read:

While Jesus was on earth, He spent a lot of time praying to God. Read Matthew 26:36 and Mark 14:32. These two verses in the Bible tell us about one of Jesus' favorite places to pray—the Garden of Gethsemane. Sometimes He chose to pray in a quiet place like the garden so that He could be alone and talk to God easily.

Because of our relationship with Jesus, we get to pray to God too! And no matter where we are, God hears us.

Think:

1. Have you prayed in any of the same places where Peter tried to pray?

2. Where is your favorite place to pray? Why?

3. How is praying different than talking to your friends? How is it the same?

4. Can you name ten different places where you could pray each day? Count them on your fingers.

5. Did you know there are different types of prayers? Think about if God has heard these prayers from you:

   - A prayer that says "thank You" to God
   - A prayer asking God to help someone else
   - A prayer asking God for His blessing or protection
   - A prayer that praises God and says "I love You" to Him
   - A prayer that says "I'm sorry"

6. Use the Prayer Poster and stickers in this book to write down your prayers and keep track of God's answers!

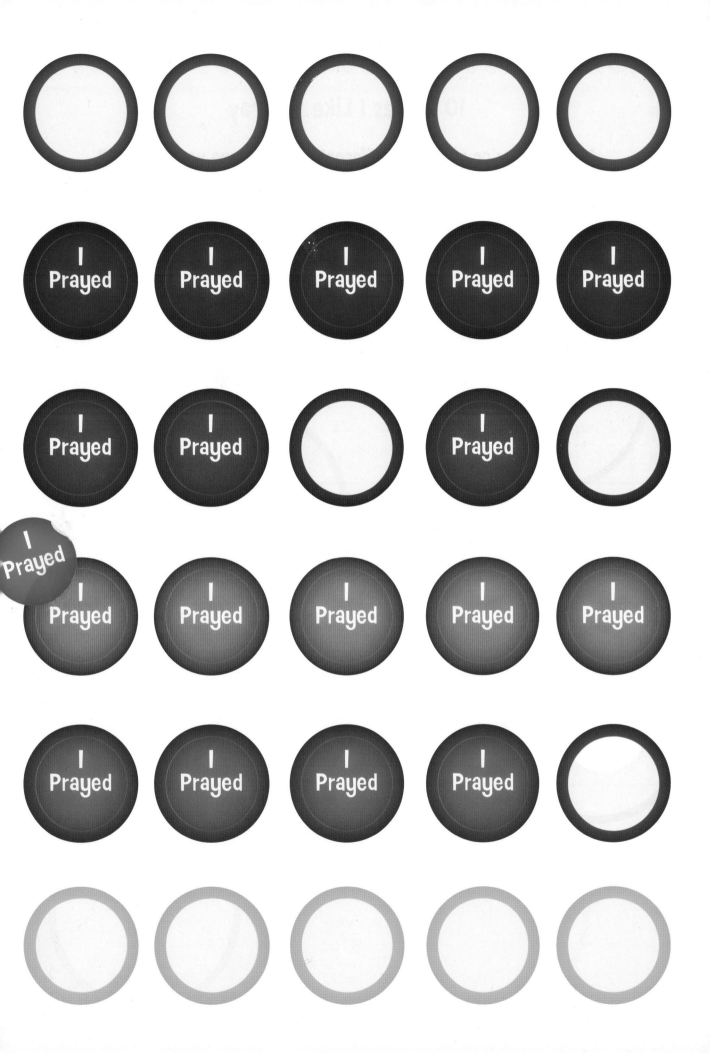

10 Places I Like to Pray

Can you draw or name ten different places where you can pray?

I Prayed

10 People I Like to Pray For

Can you draw or name ten different people you pray for?